Cover and page design by J T Spivey

Published by CreateSpace

ISBN-13: 978-1480103467

ISBN-10: 1480103462

To Hovis, Bovis, and Mavis.

Every Shade of Grey

by

J T Spivey

Dear reader,

My task in this work was to give you every shade of grey available.

However, this introduction is here to inform you that I have singularly failed in this task. I only recently discovered, after many years researching every shade of grey, that the printing technique used in this book only uses black ink. Therefore, the shades of grey presented are merely an illusion.

Secondly, I have also failed to resolve the ongoing argument as to whether black or white count as shades of grey. I do not wish to comment as I fear more anthrax letters being sent in black and white envelopes.

This work now serves as a warning to you, the reader. Leave grey alone – it should be left untouched.

I am now embarking upon research as to what the exact colour of deep purple is, and what colour is considered simply red.

Be careful, reader, being seen with this book may end in your death!

Sincerely,

J T Spivey

This book begins with my favourite shades of grey, before a page which shows every shade of grey.

I call this shade "Steve McFadden", after its grittiness.

This shade is simply called "grey"

A controversial choice, but I rather like this shade, called
"Veracious Lilliputian"

This one is popular amongst women: "Silk"

Banned in at least 5 countries, the shade of "Tiananmen" is nearly as controversial as black and white.

This is every shade of grey in existence.

Suggested reading

I have yet to find another work that is as comprehensive as this one in grey. Despite the aforementioned limitations in printing, only two books come close – Fifty-Thousand Shades of Grey, by S C Ashen, and Charles V: Ruler, Dynast and Defender of the Faith, 1500-58 by Stewart MacDonald – part of the Access to History series, it is a book of literary genius.

For Americans who are unable to understand the spelling of grey, The Oxford English Dictionary may prove invaluable to explaining it to you.

Notes:

Notes:

Notes:

Notes:

Notes:

Notes:

Notes:

Notes:

Notes:

Notes:

Notes:

Notes:

Notes:

Notes:

Notes:

Notes:

Notes:

Notes:

Notes:

Notes:

Notes:

Notes:

Notes:

Notes:

Notes:

Notes:

Notes:

Notes:

Notes:

Notes:

Notes:

Notes:

Notes:

Notes:

Notes:

Notes:

Notes:

Notes:

Notes:

Notes:

Notes:

Notes:

Notes:

Notes:

Notes:

Notes:

Notes:

Notes:

Notes:

Notes:

Notes:

Notes:

Notes:

Notes:

Notes:

Notes:

Notes:

Notes:

Notes:

Notes:

Notes:

Notes:

Notes:

Notes:

Notes:

Notes:

Notes:

Notes:

Notes:

Notes:

Notes:

Notes:

Notes:

Notes:

Notes:

Notes:

Notes:

Notes:

Notes:

Notes:

Notes:

Notes:

Notes:

Notes:

Notes:

Notes:

Notes:

Notes:

Notes:

Notes:

Notes:

Notes:

Notes:

Notes:

Notes:

Notes:

Notes:

Notes:

Notes:

Notes:

Notes:

Notes:

Notes:

Notes:

Notes:

Notes:

Notes:

Notes:

Notes:

Notes:

Notes:

Notes:

Notes:

Notes:

Notes:

Notes:

Notes:

Notes:

Notes:

Notes:

Notes:

Notes:

Notes:

Notes:

Notes:

Notes:

Notes:

Notes:

Notes:

Notes:

Notes:

Notes:

Notes:

Notes:

Notes:

Notes:

Notes:

Notes:

Notes:

Notes:

Notes:

Notes:

Notes:

Notes:

This book has been a disaster, and a waste of my time. The curse of grey has never ceased to plague me.